This Book Belongs To :
....

A
Apatosaurus

LENGTH: 21 – 23 M

MASS: 16,000 – 22,000 KG

EATS: PUZZLEGRASS

EATEN BY: TORVOSAURUS

LIVED: 161.2 – 145 MILLION YEARS AGO

Apatosaurus

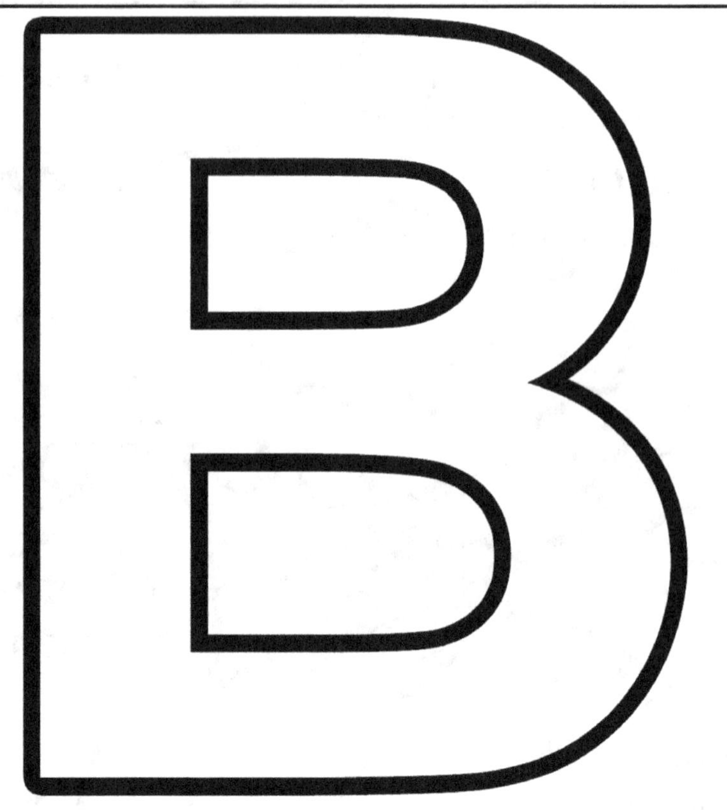

Brachiosaurus

LENGTH: 26 – 30 M

EATS: GINKGO

EATEN BY: ALLOSAURUS, TORVOSAURUS

LIVED: 161.2 – 145 MILLION YEARS AGO

Brachiosaurus
4

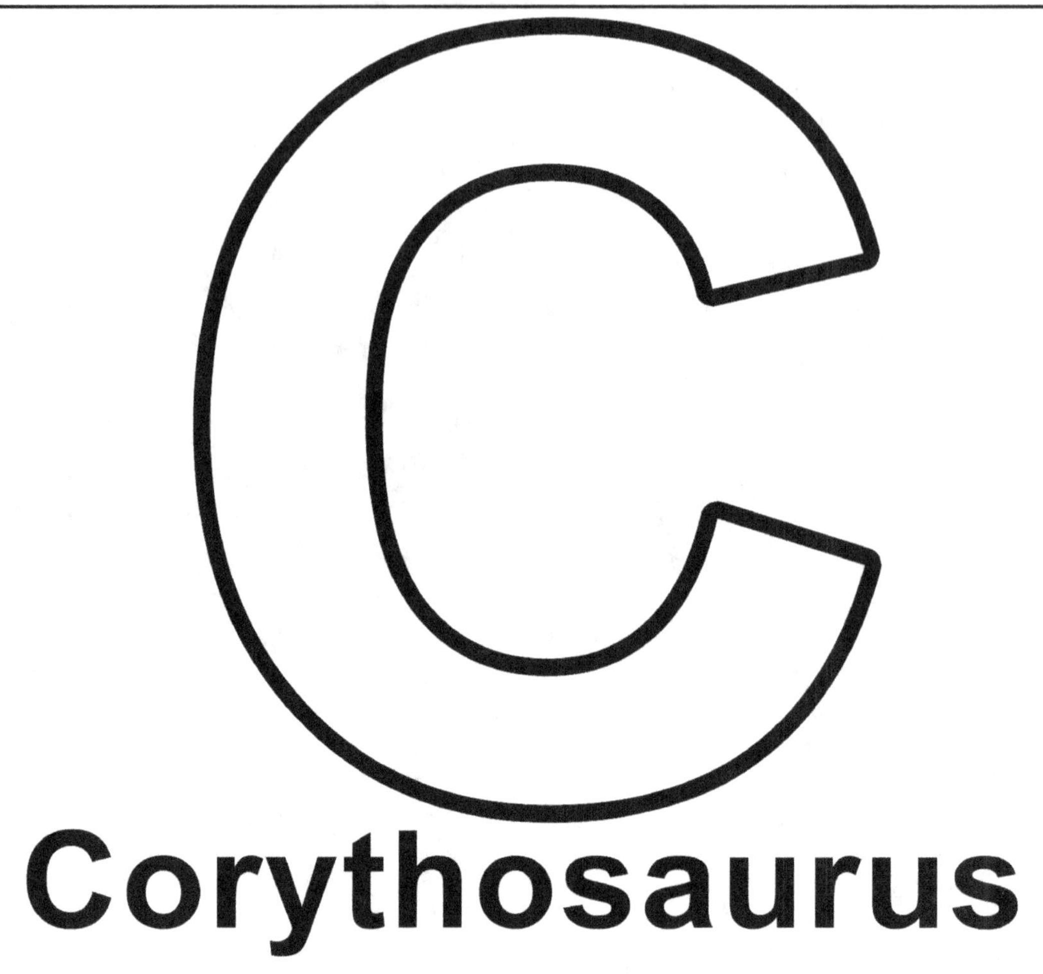

Corythosaurus

LENGTH: 7.5 – 10 M

HEIGHT: 2 M

MASS: 3,100 – 5,000 KG

LIVED: 83.6 – 70.6 MILLION YEARS AGO

Corythosaurus
6

Dimetrodon

LIVED: 295 – 272 MILLION YEARS AGO

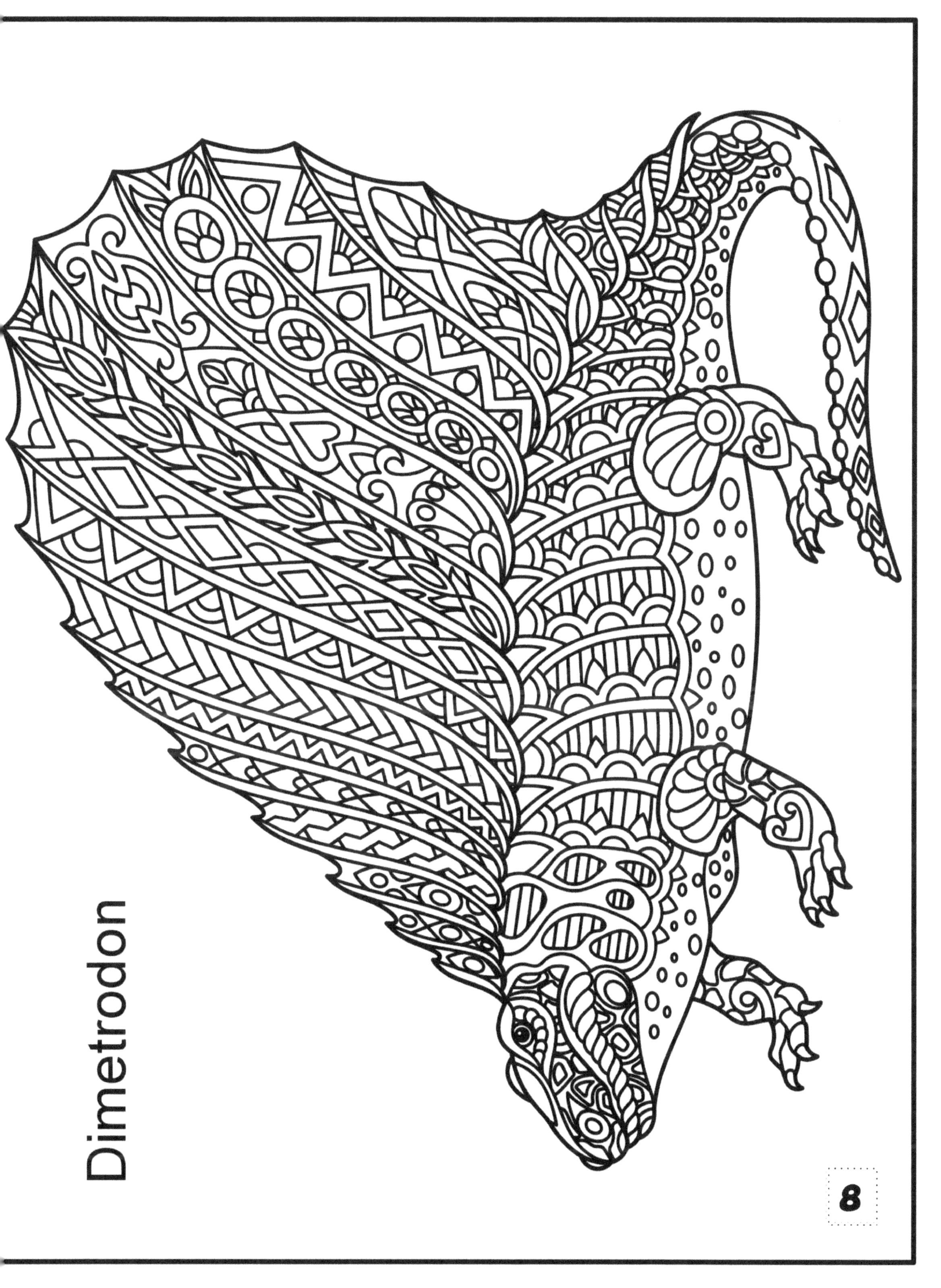

Dimetrodon

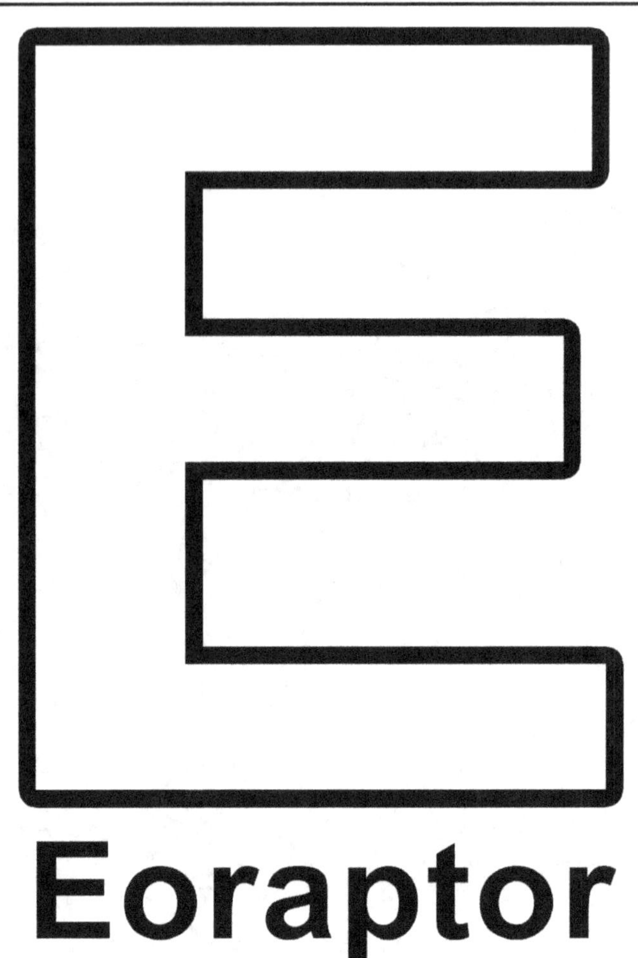

Eoraptor

LENGTH: 100 CM

MASS: 10 KG

LIVED: 237 – 228 MILLION YEARS AGO

Eoraptor

Fabrosaurus

LENGTH: 100 CM

LIVED: 199 – 189 MILLION YEARS AGO

Fabrosaurus
12

Giganotosaurus

LENGTH: 12 – 13 M

MASS: 4,200 – 14,000 KG

SPEED: 50 KM/H

EATS: ARGENTINOSAURUS, SAUROPOD

LIVED: 99.6 – 93.5 MILLION YEARS AGO

Giganotosaurus
14

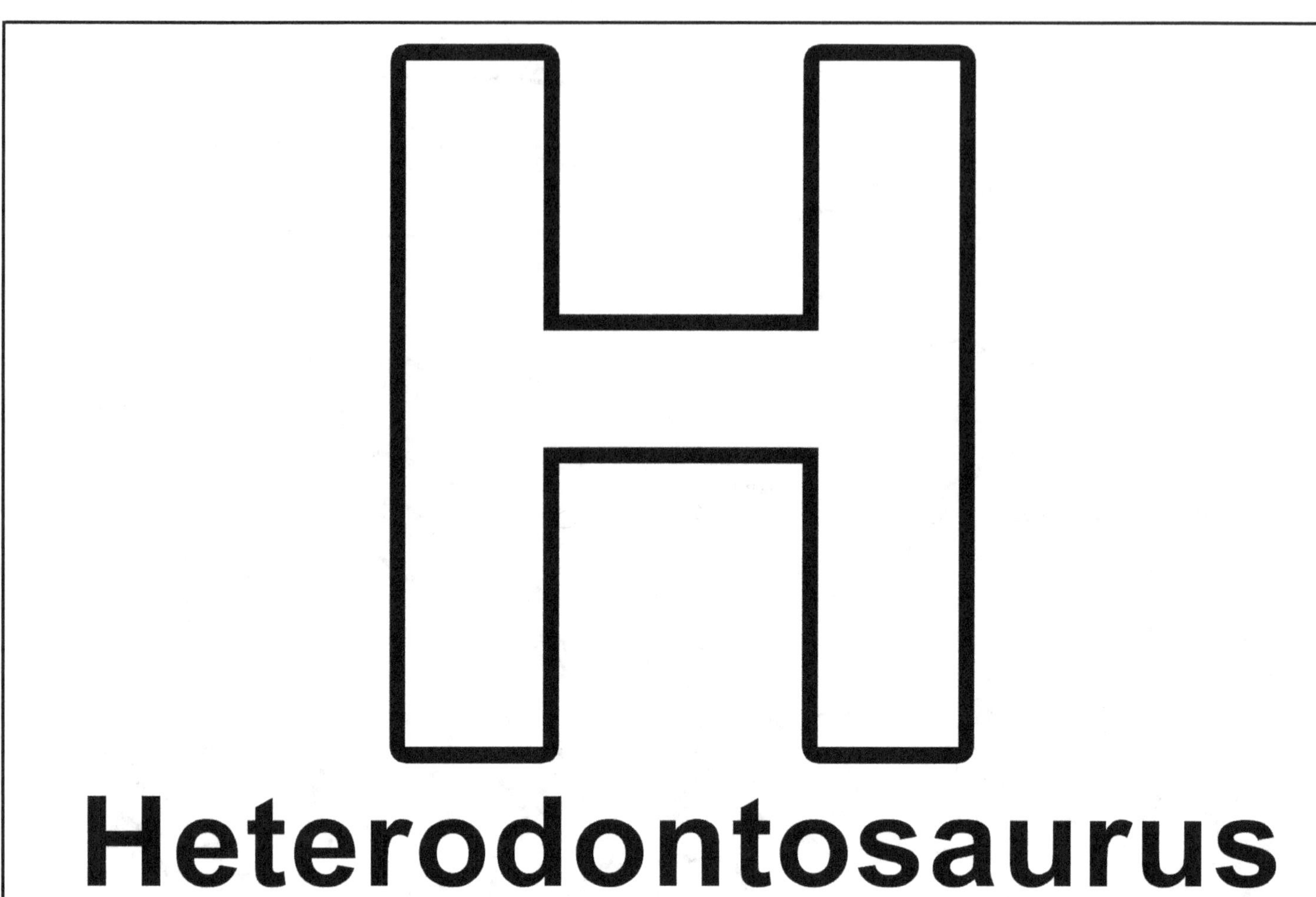

Heterodontosaurus

LENGTH: 1.2 M

MASS: 6 KG

LIVED: 228 – 182.7 MILLION YEARS AGO

Heterodontosaurus
16

Iguanodon

LENGTH: 10 m

HEIGHT: 2.7 m

MASS: 4,000 – 5,000 kg

EATS: GINKGO

LIVED: 157.3 – 93.9 MILLION YEARS AGO

Iguanodon

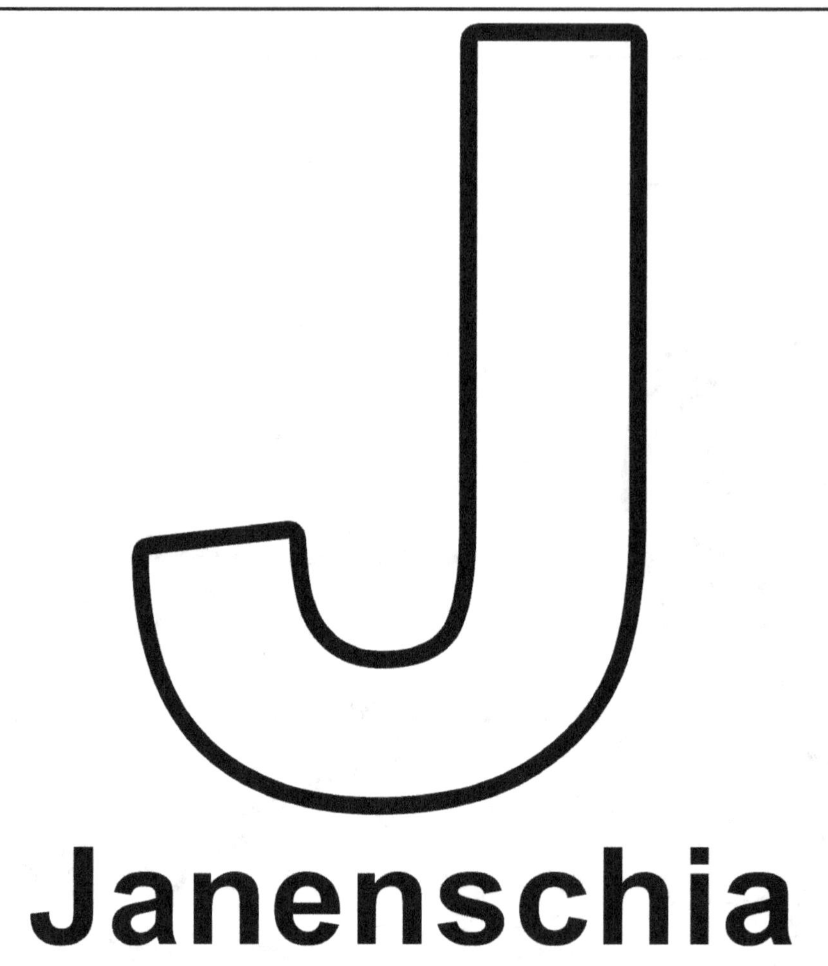

Janenschia

MASS: 10,000 – 30,000 KG

LIVED: 155.7 – 145 MILLION YEARS AGO

Janenschia
20

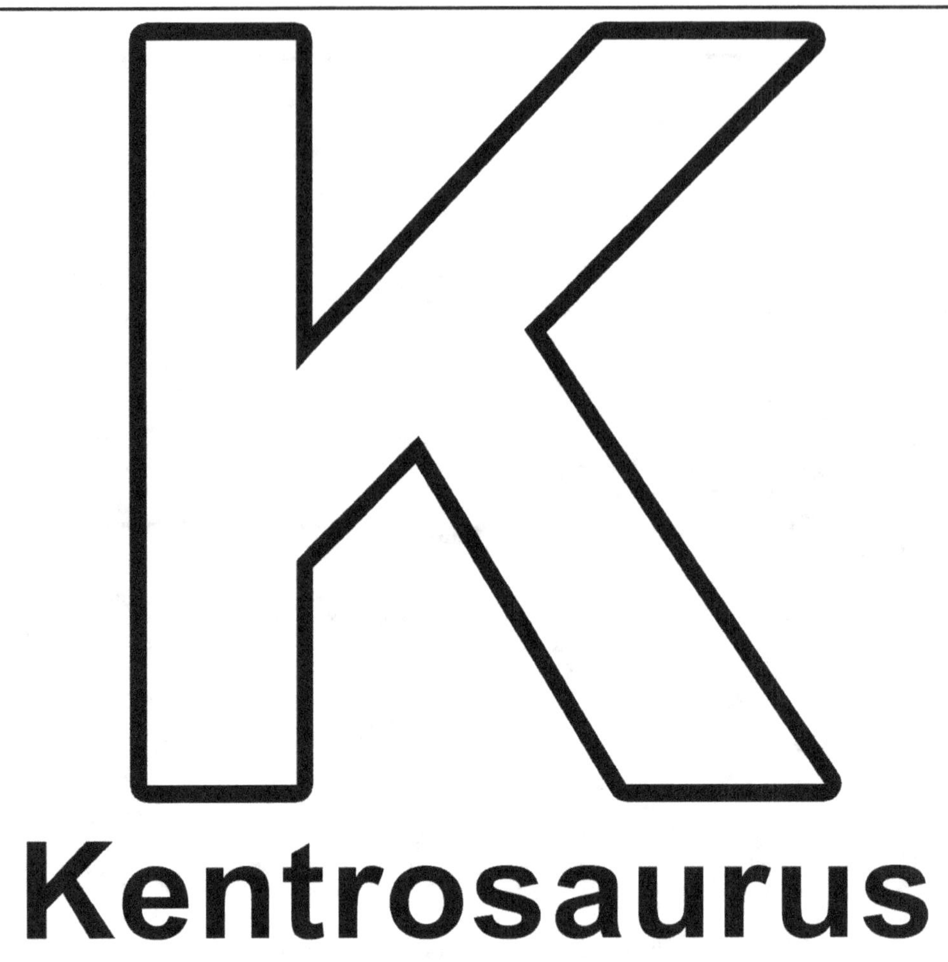

Length: 4.5 m

Mass: 1,000 – 3,000 kg

Lived: 163.5 – 145 million years ago

Kentrosaurus
22

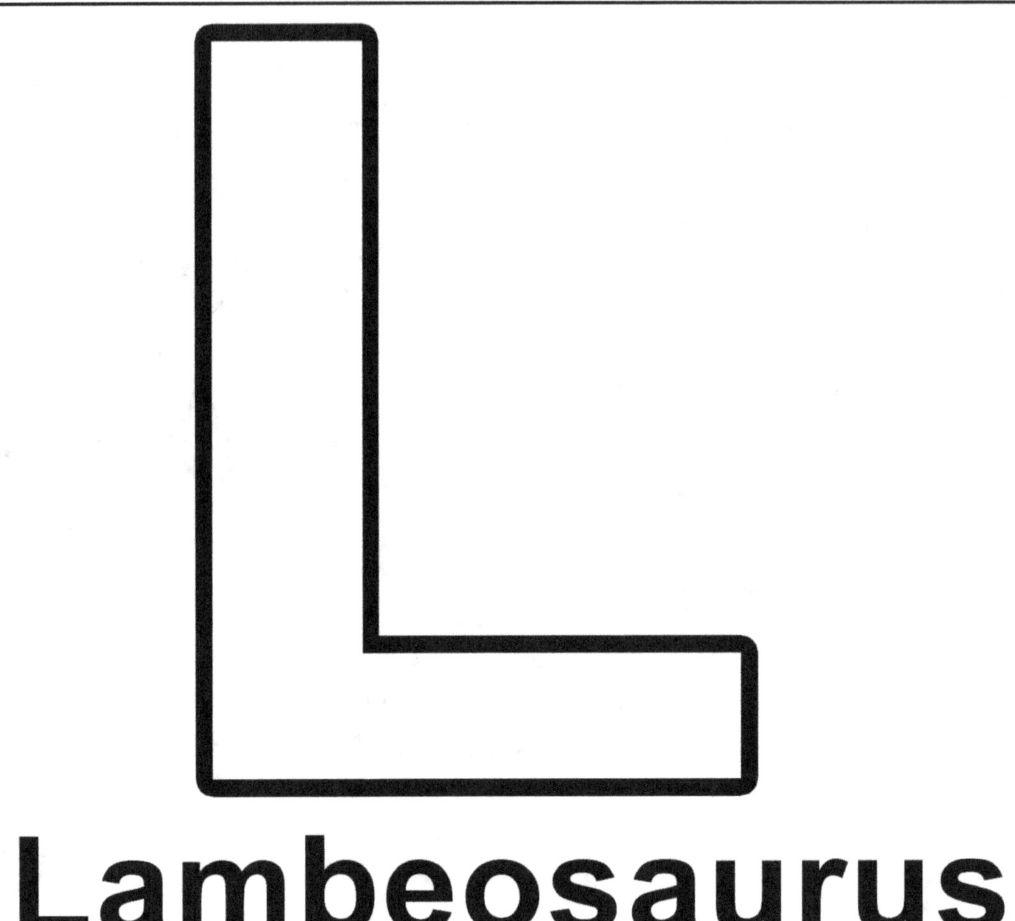

Lambeosaurus

HEIGHT: 2.1 M

LENGTH: 9 – 15 M

MASS: 1,000 – 3,000 KG

EATS: MAGNOLIA, MAIDENHAIR TREE, PINE

EATEN BY: ALBERTOSAURUS, DASPLETOSAURUS

Lambeosaurus
24

Maiasaura

HEIGHT: 2.5 M

MASS: 3,000 – 10,000 KG

LIVED: 86.3 – 70.6 MILLION YEARS AGO

Maiasaura

26

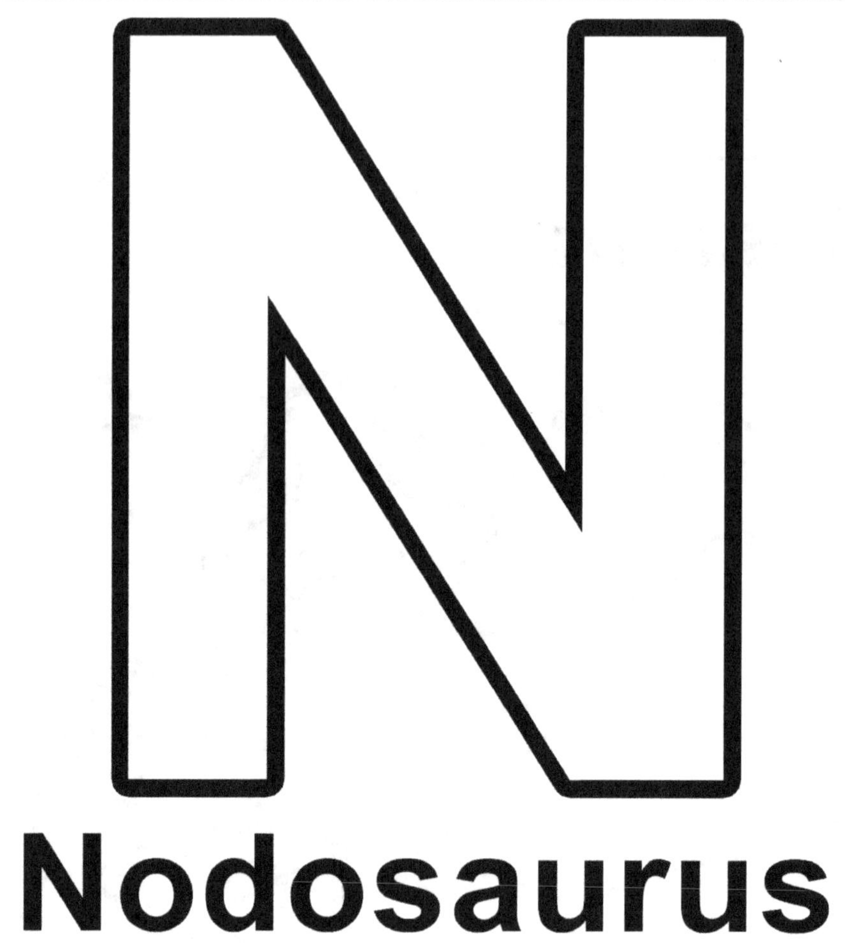

Nodosaurus

LENGTH: 4 – 6 M

LIVED: 99.6 – 70.6 MILLION YEARS AGO

Nodosaurus
28

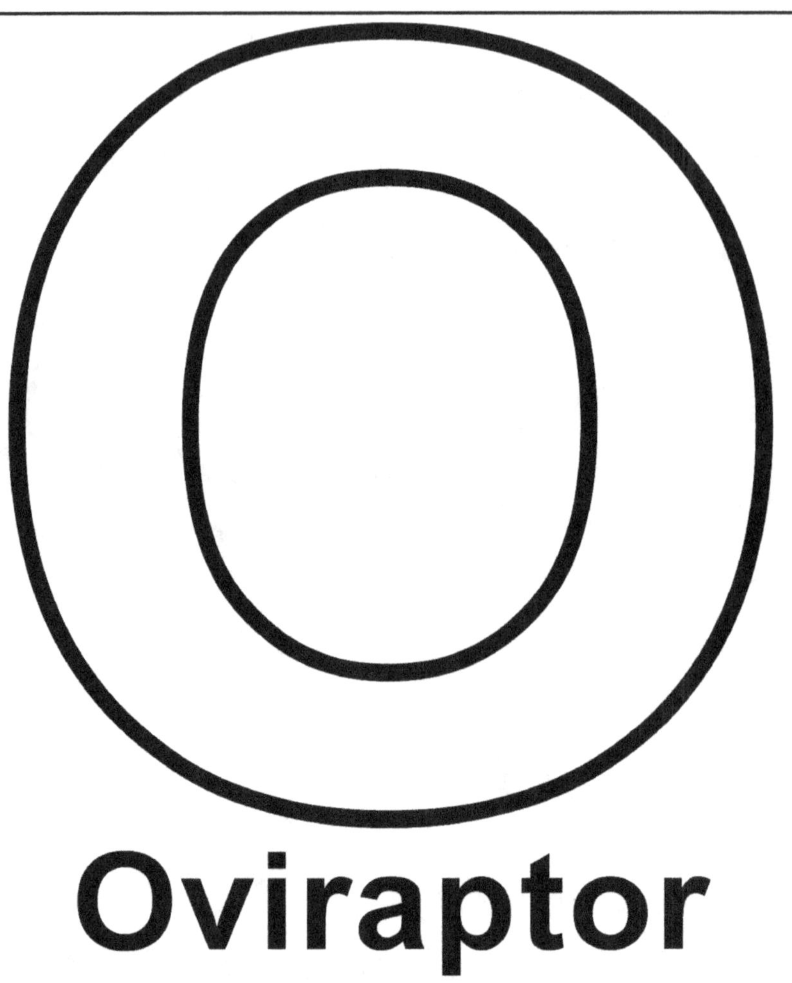

Oviraptor

HEIGHT: 91 – 150 CM

LENGTH: 1.5 M

MASS: 25 – 36 KG

SPEED: 69 KM/H

LIVED: 89.8 – 70.6 MILLION YEARS AGO

Oviraptor

Plesiosaurus

HEIGHT: 100 CM

LENGTH: 3.5 M

MASS: 450 KG

LIVED: 208.5 – 66 MILLION YEARS AGO

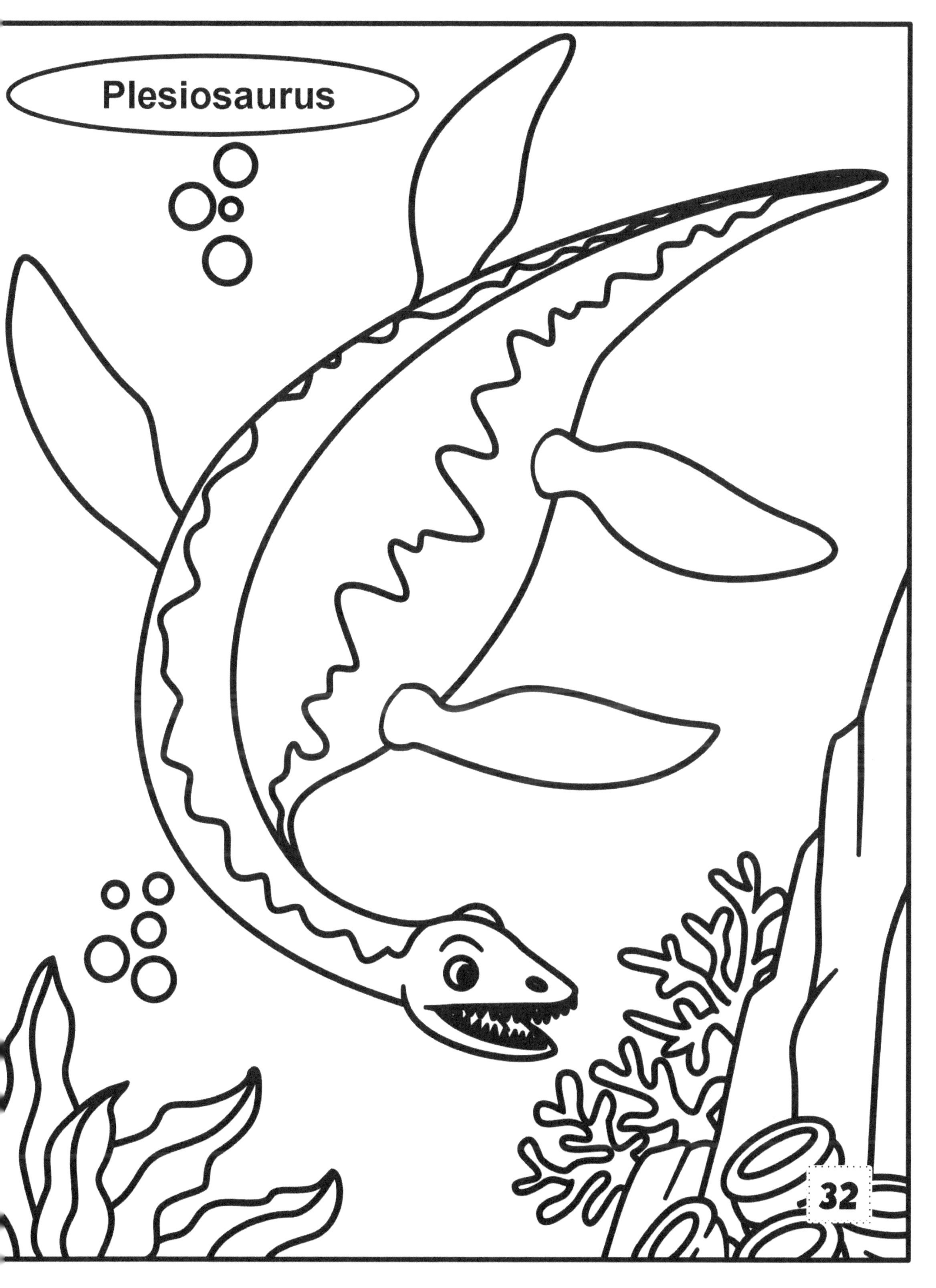
Plesiosaurus

Quaesitosaurus

LENGTH: 23 M

LIVED: 83.6 – 72.1 MILLION YEARS AGO

Quaesitosaurus

Riojasaurus

LENGTH: 10 M

MASS: 1,000 – 3,000 KG

LIVED: 228 – 208.5 MILLION YEARS AGO

Riojasaurus
36

Stegosaurus

SPEED: 7 KM/H

EATS: CYCAD, MOSS

EATEN BY: ALLOSAURUS, CERATOSAURUS

LIVED: 163.5 – 100.5 MILLION YEARS AGO

Stegosaurus
38

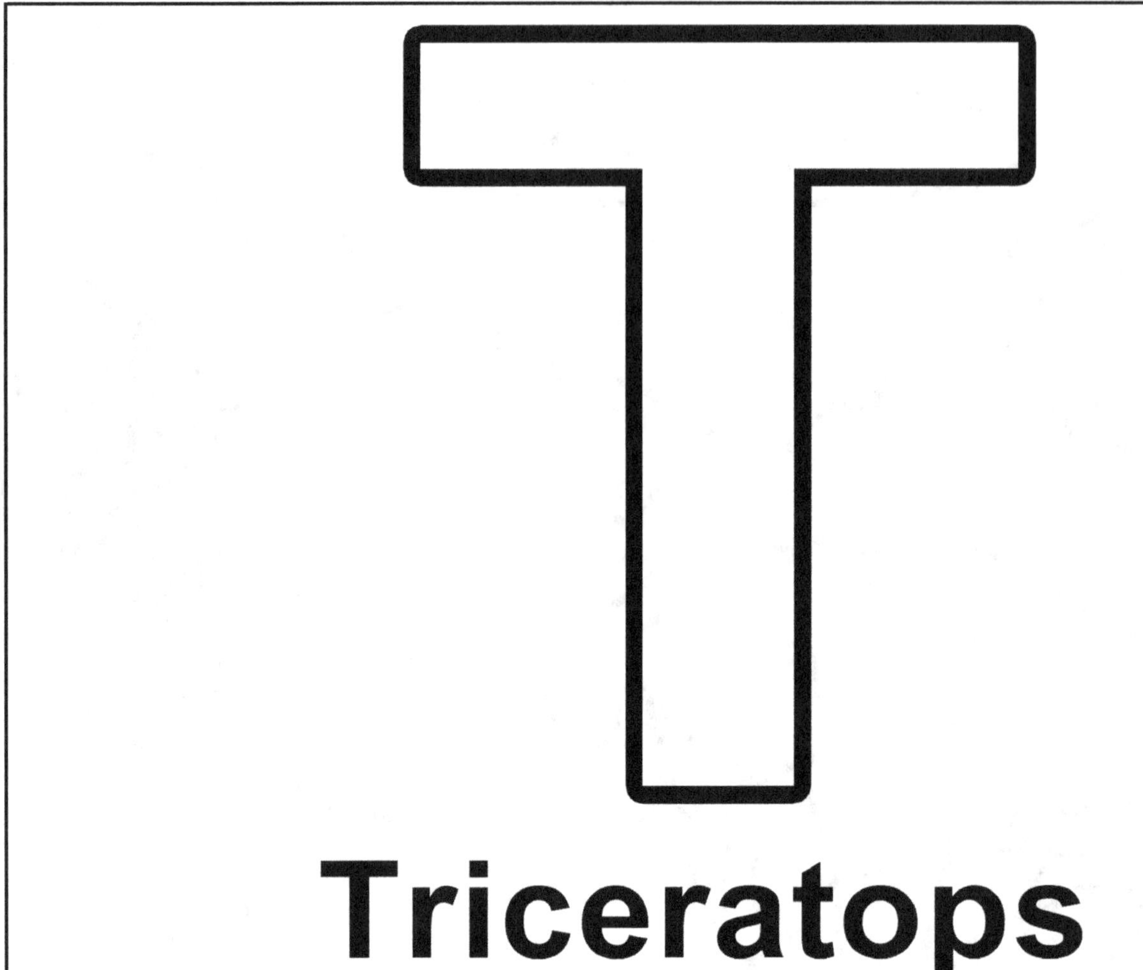

Triceratops

HEIGHT: 2.9 – 3 M

MASS: 6,000 – 12,000 KG

EATS: CYCAD, PALM TREES

EATEN BY: TYRANNOSAURUSO

LIVED: 83.5 – 66 MILLION YEARS AGO

Triceratops
40

Unenlagia

LENGTH: 2 – 3.5 M

LIVED: 93.5 – 85.8 MILLION YEARS AGO

Unenlagia
42

Velociraptor

SPEED: 64 KM/H

EATS: PROTOCERATOPS, SHUVUUIA

LIVED: 100.5 – 66 MILLION YEARS AGO

Velociraptor
44

Wannanosaurus

LENGTH: 60 CM

LIVED: 70.6 – 66 MILLION YEARS AGO

Wannanosaurus
46

Xiaosaurus

LENGTH: 100 CM

LIVED: 170.3 – 163.5 MILLION YEARS AGO

Xiaosaurus

48

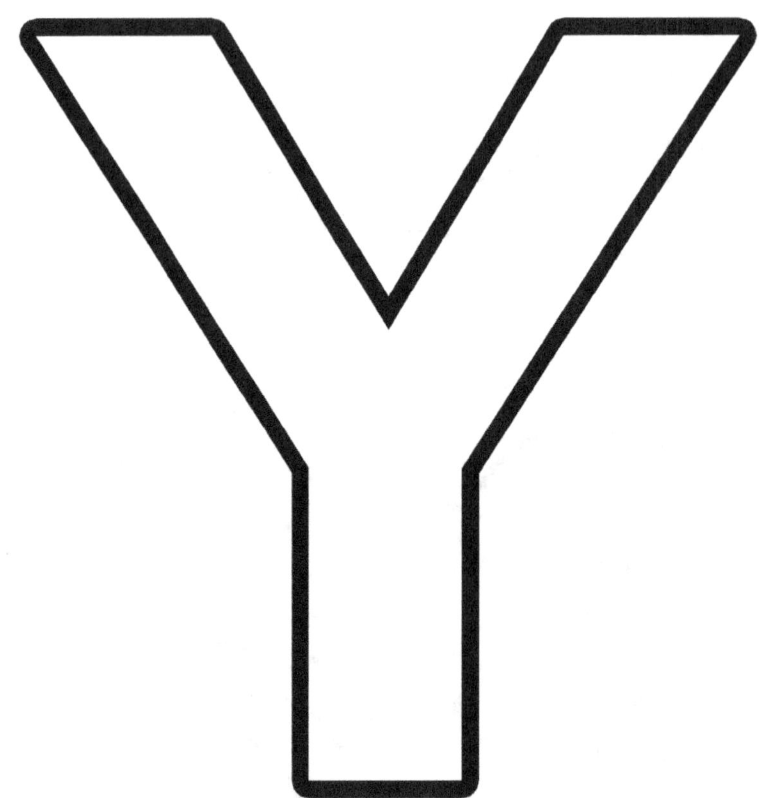

Yangchuanosaurus

LENGTH: 8 – 11 M

MASS: 1,000 – 3,000 KG

LIVED: 170.3 – 145 MILLION YEARS AGO

Yangchuanosaurus
50

Zuniceratops

LENGTH: 3 – 3.5 M

HEIGHT: 100 CM

MASS: 100 – 150 KG

LIVED: 93.5 – 89.3 MILLION YEARS AGO

52